WELCOME HOME

WELCOME HOME

A FAITH JOURNEY *for* WOMEN OVER 50

REBUILDING FAITH WITHOUT LABELS

PAULA-JEAN D'ARRIGO

WELCOME HOME

This book is a work of spiritual reflection. The views expressed are those of the author and are intended for personal encouragement and contemplation. This book is not intended to replace professional counseling, therapy, or medical advice.

ISBN: 979-8-9953704-0-6

Book designed by Mark Karis

Printed in the United States of America

CONTENTS

A PERSONAL WORD

I DID NOT SET OUT TO LEAVE THE CHURCH.

Like many women over 50, my faith was formed early and woven deeply into my life. I learned the rituals, the prayers, the discipline. Faith was present everywhere—and yet, for much of my life, it did not feel relational. It felt evaluative. It felt like something I was always trying to get right.

Prayer often felt centered on penance rather than presence. Scripture was read, but rarely opened in a way that touched my lived experience. I carried guilt, discipline, and an underlying sense that I never quite measured up—especially as a woman, navigating real life in a faith framework that often felt disconnected from reality.

Over time, I realized something honest and unsettling: I believed in Jesus, but I did not feel I was in relationship with Him. That realization did not make me rebellious. It made me tired.

When I eventually walked away, I did not feel free. I felt lost. I longed for spiritual connection, for meaningful conversation, for a place where faith could breathe. For many years, I called myself "spiritual but not religious," not because I had lost faith, but because I had lost a place where my faith felt safe.

What I never lost was belief in Jesus, prayer—both formal and informal—moral seriousness, a desire for community, and a quiet sense of God's nearness.

Years later, in a season of spiritual dryness common among women over 50, I found myself standing in a church asking for prayer. I admitted simply that I felt lost. The pastor did not question me or correct me. She looked at me and said two words that changed everything:

Welcome home.

Those words were not about a building or a denomination. They were about belonging. They named what my heart had been longing for—a faith rooted in relationship, Scripture that speaks to real life, and community shaped by grace rather than performance.

This book is for women like me.

Women who did not lose their faith, but lost their sense of belonging. Women who are spiritually wounded, cautious, hopeful, and still open. Women who are rebuilding faith without labels and discovering that coming home is less about returning to something old and more about receiving something new.

If you are reading this and thinking, *I still believe, but I feel lost*, I want you to know this:

You are not broken. You are not late. And you are not alone. Let's walk this road together.

A SPECIAL NOTE

Each chapter of this book builds on the one before it. You do not need to rush or resolve anything as you read. This is not a book about fixing faith; it is about noticing where faith is already stirring. Take your time. Pause when you need to. Let what resonates stay.

1

WHEN FAITH FEELS LIKE RULES INSTEAD OF RELATIONSHIP

FOR MANY WOMEN OVER 50, faith did not begin as a choice. It was inherited—woven into childhood, family life, and identity. We learned when to stand, when to kneel, what to say, and what not to question. Faith was present everywhere, yet relationship often felt nowhere.

Looking back, many women describe their early formation as

deeply ritualistic but thin on understanding. Scripture was read, but rarely explained in a way that touched real life. Prayer focused heavily on penance, self-examination, and correction. God felt watchful rather than welcoming.

Over time, a quiet message settled into the heart: *Try harder. Be better. Don't fail.*

For women especially, the weight of this message compounded. Teachings about womanhood, marriage, sexuality, sacrifice, and obedience often felt disconnected from lived reality. Instead of feeling accompanied, many felt measured—against rules they could never quite fulfill.

Pastoral encounters, when they came during moments of vulnerability, sometimes felt corrective rather than compassionate. Scripture was used to instruct behavior rather than to reveal the heart of Jesus. The Gospel, though beautiful in theory, did not yet feel personal or alive.

And so faith became associated with:

guilt instead of grace
discipline instead of delight
shame instead of safety
performance instead of presence.

Many women did not stop believing in God during this season. They simply never felt they were *in relationship* with Him. Jesus was known as a figure of reverence, but not yet as a companion.

This gap matters. Because when faith lacks relationship, it eventually lacks oxygen.

For many women over 50, this realization did not arrive in youth, but later—often during a season of spiritual dryness.

Children grew up. Life slowed down. Questions surfaced that had long been buried under responsibility and routine. And the old structures no longer held.

Walking away, when it happened, was rarely dramatic. It was quiet. It felt like loss. And it often left women spiritually disoriented—believing in Jesus, praying in private, longing for community, yet unsure where they belonged.

What was missing was not faith itself. What was missing was relationship.

SCRIPTURE REFLECTION

> *"Come to me, all you who are weary and burdened, and I will give you rest."*
>
> (MATTHEW 11:28)

Jesus does not begin with correction. He begins with invitation.

This chapter is not about blame. It is about naming reality—gently and honestly. Because naming is often the first step toward healing.

PERSONAL REFLECTION

When did faith begin to feel heavy rather than life-giving for you?

What messages about God did you absorb that may not reflect the heart of Jesus?

Where might God be inviting you—not to try harder, but to come closer?

THE EMMAUS ROAD

THIS JOURNEY MIRRORS THE LIVED EXPERIENCE OF MANY WOMEN OVER 50:

Walking away disappointed, confused, and spiritually dry—Still talking about God, even while feeling distant from Him—Being met by Jesus without recognition, pressure, or correction—Having Scripture opened in a new way that finally connects to lived experience—Hearing belonging before belief clarity: "Stay with us"—Returning changed—not to the same place, but with a burning heart.

2

WALKING AWAY WITHOUT LOSING JESUS

WHEN EFFORT IS NO LONGER ENOUGH

When faith feels heavy for too long, something has to give. For many women over 50, what gave way was not belief, but belonging. This chapter begins where the previous one leaves off—with honest fatigue and the quiet courage it takes to step back.

FOR MANY WOMEN OVER 50, walking away from the Church did not feel like freedom. It felt like disorientation. It felt like losing a map without losing the desire to travel.

This distinction matters.

Most women did not walk away because they stopped believing in Jesus. They walked away because they could no longer reconcile what they were experiencing internally with what they were being offered externally. Faith, as it had been practiced, no longer made room for questions, grief, complexity, or lived experience.

And yet—belief remained.

Many women continued to pray, even if the prayers were quieter and less formal. They still sensed God's nearness in moments of need, beauty, or desperation. They carried moral seriousness, a longing to live rightly, and a deep desire for meaningful community.

What they lost was not God. What they lost was *belonging*.

This is the space many women occupied for years—sometimes decades—describing themselves as "spiritual but not religious." It was not a rejection of faith, but a holding pattern. A way to stay open without being hurt again. A way to survive spiritually while avoiding spaces that felt shaming, corrective, or unsafe.

For women who had been spiritually wounded, this distance was often necessary. Wounds need air before they can bear weight. Stepping back was not abandonment—it was preservation.

The Gospel itself gives language for this season.

On the road to Emmaus, two disciples are walking away from Jerusalem. Away from community. Away from hope as they understood it. Jesus does not stop them. He joins them.

> *"Jesus himself came up and walked along with them, but they were kept from recognizing him."*
>
> (LUKE 24:15–16)

How many women over 50 recognize this moment?

God present, but unrecognized. Faith alive, but unnamed. Hope quiet, but not extinguished.

During these years, many women still spoke with God honestly.

They asked hard questions. They grieved what had been lost. They longed for a place where Scripture would finally make sense—not as instruction alone, but as relationship.

Walking away did not end the journey. It simply changed the road.

And on that road, even when it did not feel like it, Jesus was already walking beside them.

SCRIPTURE REFLECTION

"Where can I go from your Spirit? Where can I flee from your presence?"

(PSALM 139:7)

There is no season of distance that places us beyond God's reach.

PERSONAL REFLECTION

What did walking away make possible for you spiritually?

In what ways did you experience God's nearness even outside formal church life?

Where might Jesus have been walking beside you without being recognized?

3

SCRIPTURE COMES ALIVE

DISTANCE IS NOT THE END OF THE STORY

Seasons of distance often prepare the heart for deeper encounter. What felt like wandering was sometimes an unrecognized invitation. This chapter explores what happens when Scripture is finally opened in a way that speaks to real life and real wounds.

FOR MANY WOMEN OVER 50, encountering Scripture in a new environment felt like meeting a familiar person for the first time.

The Bible had always been present. Verses were read aloud, passages proclaimed, and stories repeated year after year. Yet for many women, Scripture had remained distant—respected, but not understood; heard, but not integrated.

Often, Scripture had been presented primarily as instruction: what to do, what not to do, how to behave, how to repent. Rarely was it opened slowly, relationally, or in conversation with real life. The result was not rebellion, but disconnection.

Then something changed.

For many women, it happened when Scripture was finally taught in a way that honored lived experience. The Bible was no longer used to correct from a distance, but to invite from within. Context mattered. Questions were welcomed. Stories were allowed to breathe.

Passages began to sound different—not because the words had changed, but because the posture had.

Women began to see themselves in the stories:—in the Samaritan woman, questioned yet dignified—in Martha, faithful yet misunderstood—in Mary Magdalene, devoted yet misjudged—in the unnamed women Jesus healed without interrogation.

Scripture no longer spoke at them. It spoke to them.

And more than that—it revealed Jesus not as distant authority, but as present companion. A teacher who listened. A Savior who met people where they were. A Lord whose words carried both truth and tenderness.

"The Word became flesh and made his dwelling among us."

(JOHN 1:14)

For women who had carried shame, guilt, or spiritual wounds, this mattered deeply. Scripture did not minimize holiness—it reframed it. Holiness was no longer about flawless performance, but about honest relationship.

As understanding grew, so did freedom. Women began to read Scripture not asking, What am I doing wrong? but instead, What is God revealing about Himself—and about me?

This shift often marked the beginning of healing. Not because answers suddenly appeared, but because the Bible became a place of encounter rather than evaluation.

Like the disciples on the road to Emmaus, many women could finally say: *"Were not our hearts burning within us while he talked with us on the road and opened the Scriptures to us?"* (Luke 24:32)

The burning heart was not emotional manipulation.

It was recognition. Scripture, once closed, was opening. And in its opening, so was the heart.

SCRIPTURE REFLECTION

"Your word is a lamp for my feet, a light on my path."

(PSALM 119:105)

This is not a spotlight of judgment, but a light for the next step.

PERSONAL REFLECTION

When did Scripture begin to feel personal rather than procedural for you?

What stories in the Bible resonate with your lived experience now?

How might God be meeting you through His Word—not to correct you, but to accompany you?

4

WELCOME HOME

RECOGNITION CHANGES EVERYTHING

Understanding Scripture is transformative, but belonging completes the work. This chapter moves from encounter to recognition—the moment when faith shifts from effort to rest, and the heart knows it has found its way home.

SOMETIMES, coming home does not look like returning to a place. It looks like being received.

For many women over 50, the moment of recognition arrives quietly. There is no theological argument to win, no checklist to complete, no past to explain. There is simply an invitation to be seen.

For some, it happens during a prayer. For others, in a

conversation. For many, it comes at the end of a long season of feeling spiritually lost—not faithless, but unanchored.

One woman stepped forward for prayer carrying a simple, honest confession: I feel lost. Lost in faith. Lost in life. Lost at an age when she thought she should feel settled.

The response was not instruction or interrogation. It was two words.

Welcome home.

Those words carried no conditions. They did not demand an explanation of where she had been or why she had left. They did not ask her to fix anything before belonging. They simply named what her heart already knew.

And the tears came—not from shame, but from recognition. Home is not a reward for getting faith right.

Home is the place where faith can finally rest.

This is what many women over 50 discover when they encounter a community shaped by relationship rather than performance. Scripture is opened, not wielded. Prayer is offered, not prescribed. Questions are allowed. Stories are honored.

Belonging comes first. This is deeply biblical.

On the road to Emmaus, recognition does not come through explanation alone. It comes when Jesus breaks bread—a familiar, relational act. Their eyes are opened not by information, but by presence.

> *"Then their eyes were opened and they recognized him."*
>
> (LUKE 24:31)

For women who have been spiritually wounded, this matters profoundly. Wounds heal in safe places. Faith deepens where it is not rushed. Trust grows where it is not demanded.

Coming home does not erase the past. It redeems it.

The years of distance, questioning, and longing become part of the testimony—not of failure, but of faith that refused to die.

Home, in this sense, is not a building or a denomination. It is the moment when the heart says, This is what was missing.

And when that recognition comes, something shifts. Not everything is suddenly clear. But something is settled. Faith feels like a breath of fresh air. A new beginning.

SCRIPTURE REFLECTION

> *"You are no longer strangers and foreigners, but fellow citizens with God's people and members of God's household."*
>
> (EPHESIANS 2:19)

Belonging is not earned. It is given.

PERSONAL REFLECTION

When have you experienced being received without explanation or defense?

What does spiritual home mean to you now?

Where might God be inviting you to rest rather than strive?

5

RETURNING CHANGED: BECOMING A COMPANION ON THE ROAD

FOR MANY WOMEN OVER 50, coming home does not end the journey. It clarifies it.

On the Emmaus road, the disciples do not remain at the table once they recognize Jesus. They rise and return—not because they are commanded to, but because something within them has been restored. Their fear loosens its grip. Their story matters again.

"*They got up and returned at once to Jerusalem.*" (Luke 24:33) This return is not a reversal. It is a transformation.

Women who have walked through spiritual dryness, distance, and wounding do not return naïve or unquestioning. They return wise. They carry discernment, compassion, and humility that cannot be taught in classrooms or acquired through rule-following alone.

They know what it feels like to be lost—and what it feels like to be found without being shamed.

This matters because faith at this stage of life is no longer about proving devotion. It is about presence.

Many women over 50 feel an unexpected stirring: a desire not to teach from authority, but to walk alongside others. To listen without correcting. To open Scripture without weaponizing it. To create spaces where questions are not treated as threats.

This is not leadership as control. This is leadership as companionship.

Jesus sends the disciples back not with a program, but with a story. We have seen the Lord. And that is often all spiritually wounded people need to hear—not answers, but testimony.

Women who have been shaped by both faith and fracture are uniquely equipped for this work. They do not rush healing. They honor process. They recognize that belonging often precedes belief clarity.

Returning changed may look like:—hosting a small group that prioritizes safety—listening more than speaking—praying with others without prescribing solutions—opening Scripture gently and contextually—using language that heals rather than divides.

None of this requires a title. It requires presence.

For women over 50 rebuilding faith without labels, this is holy ground. Their journey becomes a bridge for others who are still walking the road—still wondering if they belong, still unsure if God is near.

The invitation is not to convince. It is to accompany. And in doing so, many women discover that the words spoken over them—Welcome home—are now words they are able to speak to others.

Not as gatekeepers. But as fellow travelers.

SCRIPTURE REFLECTION

"Praise be to the God and Father of our Lord Jesus Christ, the Father of compassion and the God of all comfort, who comforts us in all our troubles, so that we can comfort those in any trouble with the comfort we ourselves receive from God."

(2 CORINTHIANS 1:3–4)

This is not about returning to what was. It is about moving forward with what has been redeemed.

CLOSING BLESSING

You are not late. You are not broken. You are not disloyal.

You are becoming.

May your faith continue to feel like a breath of fresh air.

May your story make room for others.

And may many hearts hear the words you once needed most:

Welcome Home.

If you would like to sit with the message of this book a little longer, music can sometimes reach the heart before words do.

Search for "Come As You Are" by Crowder on your preferred music platform.

ABOUT THE AUTHOR

PAULA-JEAN D'ARRIGO is the author of *Welcome Home: A Faith Journey for Women Over 50 Rebuilding Faith Without Labels.* Drawing from her own spiritual journey, Paula-Jean writes for women who have carried faith quietly—especially those who have stepped away from formal faith practice yet continue to long for meaning, connection, and truth.

Her work centers Scripture as invitation rather than instruction, creating space for women to encounter God's Word without fear of condemnation or pressure to perform. With clarity, compassion, and deep respect for lived experience, she writes for those rebuilding faith in a way that feels relational, honest, and whole.

www.ingramcontent.com/pod-product-compliance
Lightning Source LLC
LaVergne TN
LVHW090541110826
845146LV00003B/1221

* 9 7 9 8 9 9 5 3 7 0 4 0 6 *